DECOMPOSERS
Millipedes

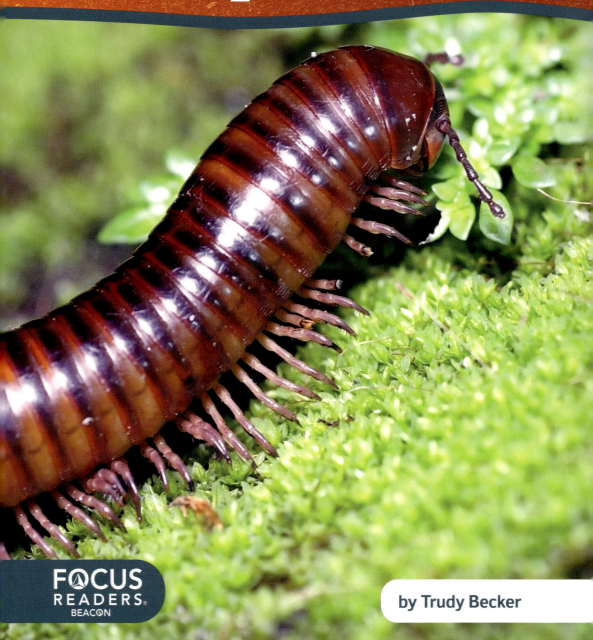

FOCUS READERS®
BEACON

by Trudy Becker

www.focusreaders.com

Copyright © 2025 by Focus Readers®, Mendota Heights, MN 55120. All rights reserved. No part of this book may be reproduced or utilized in any form or by any means without written permission from the publisher.

Focus Readers is distributed by North Star Editions: sales@northstareditions.com | 888-417-0195

Produced for Focus Readers by Red Line Editorial.

Photographs ©: iStockphoto, cover, 1, 4, 11; Shutterstock Images, 7, 8, 14, 17, 18, 22, 25, 26, 29; P. Marek, W. Shear, and J. Bond/ZooKeys, 12; National Park Service, 21

Library of Congress Cataloging-in-Publication Data
Names: Becker, Trudy, author.
Title: Millipedes / by Trudy Becker.
Description: Mendota Heights, MN: Focus Readers, [2025] | Series: Decomposers | Includes index. | Audience: Grades 2-3
Identifiers: LCCN 2024031606 (print) | LCCN 2024031607 (ebook) | ISBN 9798889984009 (hardcover) | ISBN 9798889984283 (paperback) | ISBN 9798889984825 (pdf) | ISBN 9798889984566 (ebook)
Subjects: LCSH: Millipedes--Juvenile literature.
Classification: LCC QL449.6 .B43 2025 (print) | LCC QL449.6 (ebook) | DDC 595.6/6--dc23/eng/20240710
LC record available at https://lccn.loc.gov/2024031606
LC ebook record available at https://lccn.loc.gov/2024031607

Printed in the United States of America
Mankato, MN
012025

About the Author

Trudy Becker lives in Minneapolis, Minnesota. She likes exploring new places and loves anything involving books.

Table of Contents

CHAPTER 1
A Leafy Meal   5

CHAPTER 2
Plant Decomposers   9

CHAPTER 3
New Soil   15

THAT'S AMAZING!
From Ocean to Land   20

CHAPTER 4
Keeping Balance   23

Focus Questions • 28
Glossary • 30
To Learn More • 31
Index • 32

CHAPTER 1
A Leafy Meal

The sun goes down. Nighttime falls in the forest. A leaf shifts on the forest floor. A millipede crawls out from underneath. It's ready to eat.

 Millipedes are active at night. They sleep during the day.

The millipede can smell food nearby. The creature's many legs scurry across the ground. Its **antennae** twitch. Soon, the millipede reaches a pile of leaf litter. The millipede opens its jaws. Then it begins eating the dead leaves and bark.

Did You Know?
Millipedes are born with three sets of legs. They grow more legs as they get older.

Antennae help millipedes sense the world around them.

Later, the millipede poops. The poop adds to the forest's soil. Then the sun comes back up. The millipede hides away. It will eat more tomorrow.

CHAPTER 2
Plant Decomposers

Ecosystems have three groups of life-forms. Producers make their own food. Consumers eat other living things. And decomposers break things down. Millipedes are important decomposers.

 Millipedes spend a lot of time underground.

Millipedes help break down dead material. They are herbivores. That means they eat material that comes from plants. Millipedes sometimes eat living plants. But most of their food is dead plants. They also eat soil and animal waste.

Millipedes have strong jaws. That helps millipedes bite and chew through food. And their many legs help them move through the dirt. That makes it easier to search for food.

Some millipedes feed on rotting fruits.

After millipedes eat, the dead material goes into their **digestive systems**. Other tiny life-forms live there. These often include fungi. They may also include tiny worms. These life-forms break down the

The *Illacme plenipes* millipede can have more than 600 legs.

food. Millipedes get energy from it. Then they poop. They turned the dead material into a new substance It goes back into the dirt.

More than 12,000 kinds of millipedes exist. They live across the globe. Usually, they live in cool and damp places. They also tend to stay in dark areas. For example, millipedes often hide under dirt and leaves. Forests are common habitats. So are gardens. Many millipedes can live anywhere with enough water and soil.

Did You Know?
The word *millipede* means "one thousand legs." But most millipedes have fewer than one hundred legs.

CHAPTER 3

New Soil

Millipedes survive by eating dead plant material. But their eating also helps entire ecosystems. If ecosystems had no decomposers, dead plants would pile up. So would dead parts of living plants.

 Millipedes often feed on plants that other decomposers have partly broken down.

For example, many trees lose leaves in autumn. The trees are still alive. But the leaves are dead material. They cover the ground. Millipedes help remove the dead leaves.

Millipedes also **recycle** the dead material. Plant and animal waste includes many **nutrients**. For instance, dead leaves often contain nitrogen. Living plants need that. Nitrogen in the soil helps plants grow. However, nitrogen is stuck in dead leaves. Until the leaves

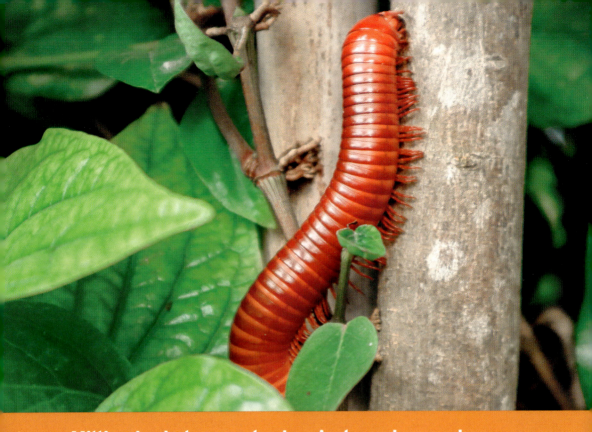

▷ **Millipedes help recycle chemicals such as carbon. Plants use carbon to grow.**

break down, other plants can't get to it. But millipedes can. They eat the dead leaves. They keep some nutrients in their bodies. Then they release the rest by pooping.

▷ **Some people keep millipedes in their gardens to help plants grow.**

Millipede poop returns nutrients to the soil. New plants can thrive in it. The poop helps plants grow better. Nutrient recycling is very important in some areas. For example, soil in dry places often lacks nutrients. It could not support plant life without millipedes.

Millipedes also change the soil's thickness. When millipedes eat dirt, they make the soil looser. That means more air can get through the soil. More water can reach plant roots, too.

Did You Know?
Many millipedes **migrate** during very wet or dry conditions. They search for damp areas.

THAT'S AMAZING!

From Ocean to Land

Millipedes are one of Earth's oldest creatures. In fact, millipedes have existed on Earth for hundreds of millions of years.

Earth's first creatures lived in the oceans. That changed over time. Some creatures moved onto land. Scientists learned about this change through **fossils**.

Many of the oldest fossils show millipedes. Millipedes used to live underwater. Then they came onto land more than 400 million years ago. That makes millipedes one of the earliest creatures on land.

▶ Scientists can use fossils to learn what life was like millions of years ago.

CHAPTER 4

Keeping Balance

Millipedes pass on nutrients that plants need to live. But millipedes do more than just help plants. They also help keep the entire **food chain** balanced.

 Some millipedes live together in groups.

For instance, many animals are herbivores. Two examples include mice and rabbits. These animals survive better when more plants grow. Other animals eat meat. They include snakes and owls. These animals hunt the herbivores. In this way, plant growth helps the whole food chain get enough to eat.

Some animals feed on millipedes, too. For example, shrews and badgers eat them. So do toads and frogs. Even some kinds of bugs

▷ Many types of birds feed on millipedes.

hunt millipedes. Millipedes are a key food for some ants, spiders, and beetles.

If **predators** ate too many millipedes, the ecosystem would be unbalanced. But fortunately, millipedes can protect themselves. Hard shells on their bodies help.

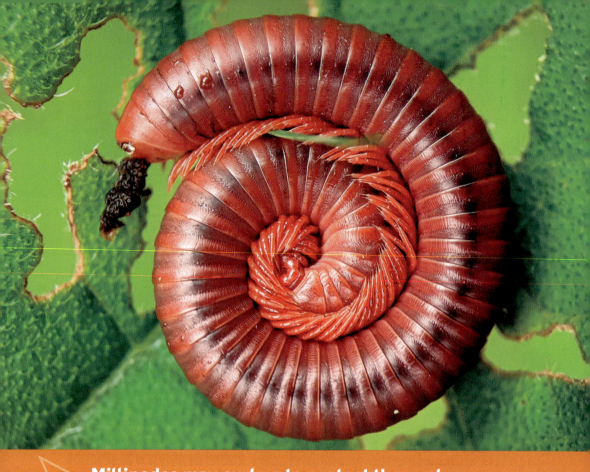

▸ **Millipedes may curl up to protect themselves.**

These shells make it harder for predators to smash millipedes. Some millipedes let out liquids when in danger. These liquids are smelly and harmful. They can make predators stop attacking. Other millipedes glow in the dark. That shows they are dangerous. Predators know to stay away.

These protections help millipedes survive. Then they can decompose more dead material. And they can keep helping the ecosystem.

Did You Know?
Millipede **venom** usually doesn't harm humans. But sometimes people get blisters or rashes.

Focus Questions

Write your answers on a separate piece of paper.

1. Write a few sentences explaining the main ideas of Chapter 2.

2. Would you want millipedes living near you? Why or why not?

3. What do millipedes mostly eat?
    - **A.** dead plants
    - **B.** living plants
    - **C.** other herbivores

4. Which of these animals is a predator?
    - **A.** a millipede
    - **B.** a rabbit
    - **C.** a frog

5. What does **habitats** mean in this book?

*Forests are common **habitats**. So are gardens. Many millipedes can live anywhere with enough water and soil.*

    A. food that animals eat
    B. areas where animals live
    C. different types of animals

6. What does **thrive** mean in this book?

*Millipede poop returns nutrients to the soil. New plants can **thrive** in it. The poop helps plants grow better.*

    A. do well
    B. do poorly
    C. do nothing

Answer key on page 32.

Glossary

antennae
Long, thin body parts on the heads of millipedes.

digestive systems
Groups of body parts that break down food into energy and nutrients.

ecosystems
The collections of living things in different natural areas.

food chain
The feeding relationships among different living things.

fossils
Parts of animals or plants that remain preserved in rock.

migrate
To move from one region to another.

nutrients
Substances that living things need to stay strong and healthy.

predators
Animals that hunt other animals for food.

recycle
To take something and turn it into something new to use.

venom
A harmful substance made by an animal.

To Learn More

BOOKS

Klepinger, Teresa. *Soil-Eating Animals*. Mendota Heights, MN: Focus Readers, 2022.

Loh-Hagan, Virginia. *Smelly Stinkers*. Ann Arbor, MI: Cherry Lake Publishing, 2023.

London, Martha. *Ecosystems*. Minneapolis: Abdo Publishing, 2022.

NOTE TO EDUCATORS

Visit **www.focusreaders.com** to find lesson plans, activities, links, and other resources related to this title.

Index

A
antennae, 6

C
consumers, 9

D
decomposers, 9, 15
digestive systems, 11

E
ecosystems, 9, 15, 25, 27

F
food chain, 23–25
fossils, 20
fungi, 11

H
habitats, 13
herbivores, 10, 24

L
leaf litter, 6
legs, 6, 10, 13

N
nitrogen, 16
nutrients, 16–19, 23

P
predators, 25–27
producers, 9
protections, 25–27

V
venom, 27